# The Tyler Graphics Archive

Kenneth Tyler pulling a proof of David Hockney's *Potted Daffodils* from a lithographic limestone.

The Tyler Graphics Archive at Walker Art Center is a richly diverse collection of more than one thousand prints by prominent contemporary painters and sculptors who, working with master printer Kenneth Tyler, have explored many new stylistic and technical directions. The Walker's collection includes one print from every edition published by Tyler Graphics Ltd. as well as a representative selection of monotypes and other one-of-a-kind works on paper. In the future, one impression from every new Tyler Graphics print edition will come to the Art Center, thus guaranteeing the continuing development of this area of the collection.

The Tyler Graphics Archive represents a spectrum of important stylistic currents, ranging from the precise geometry of Josef Albers to the intuitive expressionism of Frank Stella. The collection includes prints by notable geometric abstractionists including Ellsworth Kelly, Kenneth Noland and Jack Tworkov as well as work by leading first and second generation Abstract Expressionists such as Robert Motherwell, Helen Frankenthaler and Joan Mitchell. A number of artists who came to prominence during the 1960s, many in relation to the Pop Art movement, are also represented including David Hockney, Richard Hamilton, Malcolm Morley, Roy Lichtenstein and Claes Oldenburg. Among the sculptors who have made prints at Tyler Graphics are Anthony Caro, Mark di Suvero and Michael Heizer. Other artists in the collection are Anni Albers, Ed Baynard, Stanley Boxer, William Crutchfield, Ronald Davis, Nancy Graves, Paul Jenkins, Hugh O'Donnell, Alan Shields, Richard Smith, Steven Sorman and Robert Zakanitch.

In addition to an example of every print published by Tyler Graphics, the Archive includes sketches, maquettes, photographic documentation of work in progress, woodblocks, metal plates and various other printing elements, as well as a range of working and trial proofs used in producing each edition that offers fascinating visual records of the creative process. The Archive is a virtual compendium of printmaking techniques from intaglio, woodcut, silkscreen, lithography, letterpress and monotype to the hybrid use of these media. It is also an excellent resource for contemporary papermaking, one of Tyler's fascinations. Not only does he go to great lengths to find the paper best suited to each artist's needs, but he has established papermaking facilities on the Tyler Graphics premises. With its broad selection of prints, rare proofs and handmade paper by artists representing major stylistic currents of our time, the Tyler Graphics Archive is an invaluable collection for anyone interested in contemporary art and printmaking.

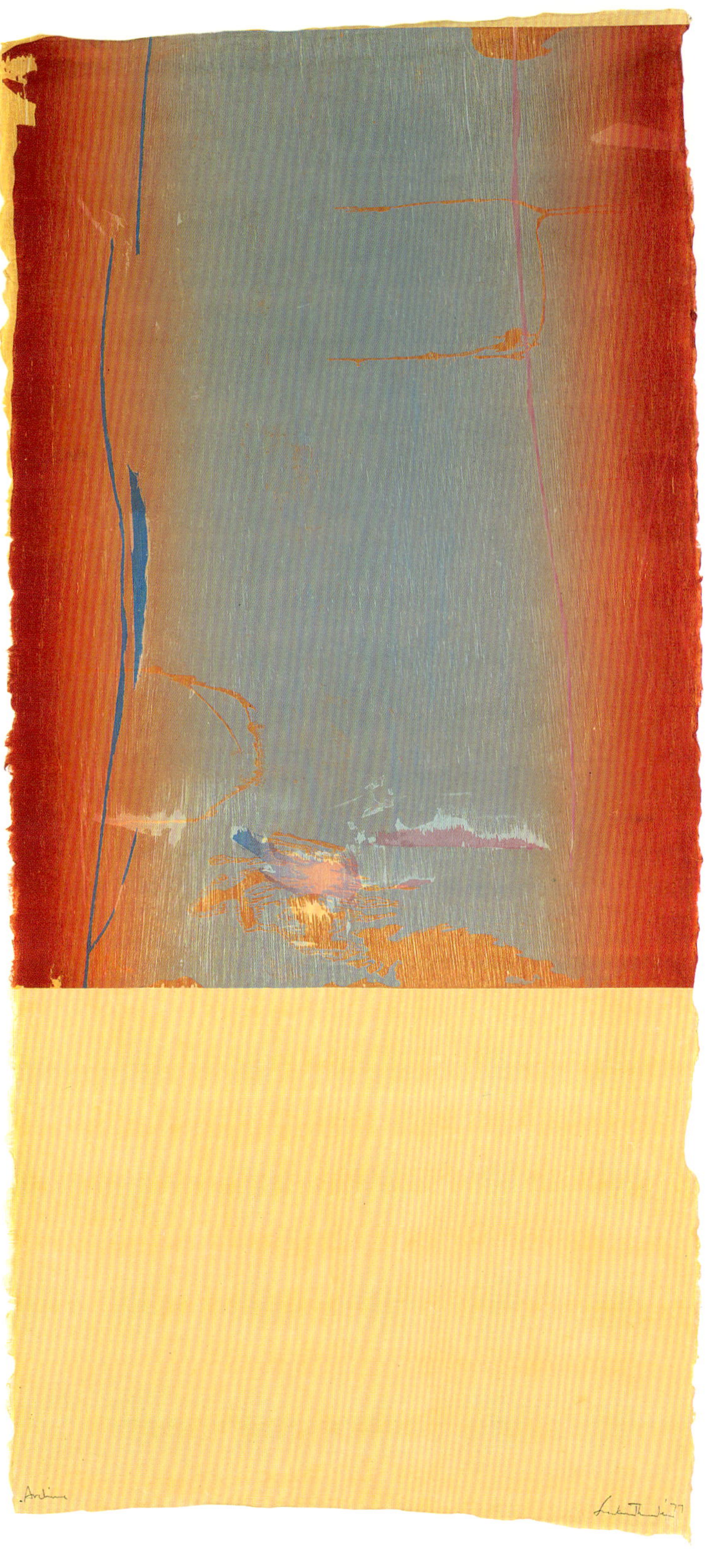

# Kenneth Tyler and the American Print Renaissance

*Elizabeth Armstrong*

An astonishing transformation has taken place in American printmaking over the past twenty-five years. From a highly specialized, somewhat timid reproductive medium it has become a highly flexible, creative form increasingly used as a primary means of expression by major contemporary artists. Behind this unprecedented print boom are a few extremely innovative, dedicated master printers who possess knowledge and skills rivaling those in print workshops throughout the world. They have provided American artists with the technical means that have powered this "print renaissance."

Always a demanding craft, printmaking today recognizes an extraordinary expertise of many individuals, including printing press designers, chemical engineers, papermaking specialists, as well as master printers. Yet such advanced technology must always remain flexible and responsive to the requirements of an artist's vision; it must be at the service of aesthetic objectives. In order to accomplish this, an energetic collaboration must exist between two individuals: the artist and the printer.

Kenneth Tyler is a master printer whose approach in the workshop exemplifies that rare combination of artistic sensibility and technical wizardry. Since the early 1960s, he has been regarded as one of this country's most dedicated proponents of the creative possibilities of printmaking. He has designed new presses, made his own paper, and engineered innovative printing techniques. At the same time, his passionate belief in the validity of the printmaking medium and his sensitivity to artists' needs has attracted major painters and sculptors to work with him in this arena. Taking an entirely open approach to printmaking, he has challenged artists to push beyond the traditional limitations of the printing process. A skillful and demanding collaborator, he has been an important catalyst in the creation of new forms and conceptions.

The transformation of printmaking from reproductive medium to unique and fully-realized artistic expression occurred relatively slowly in America. Our earliest printmakers were largely self-taught men such as Paul Revere, that all-around craftsman of the eighteenth century who, aside from his other accomplishments as silversmith, bell caster and heroic midnight courier, printed whatever was required, including pamphlets, almanacs, calendars, trade cards, propaganda and currency for the Massachusetts Bay Colony.[1] In nineteenth-century America, engravings made by printers after paintings, for example, gained a large audience. The public taste for information and decoration contributed as well to the wide popularity of Currier and Ives lithographs, idealized

(p. 6)
Helen Frankenthaler
*Essence Mulberry* 1977
woodblock print on Maniai handmade Gampi paper
39½ x 18½ edition 46

Ellsworth Kelly
*Colors on a Grid, Screenprint 1976* 1976
screenprint with lithography on Arches 88 mouldmade paper
48¼ x 48¼ edition 46

genre scenes that were advertised as "cheap engravings for the people." For the most part, painters in eighteenth- and nineteenth-century America considered printmaking a craft—not an art form. Painters were artists, printers were workers, and few crossed the divide.

In Europe, on the other hand, fine art and graphic art traditions have long co-existed. It follows that, in the early part of this century, some of the most distinctive contributions to American printmaking were made by artists trained in Europe such as Lyonel Feininger, Max Weber and Josef Albers. Not until the 1960s did America begin training its own master printers and offering artists, for the first time, the technical and collaborative resources of the printmaking workshops.

In 1957, Tatyana Grosman, who came to the U.S. in 1943, founded Universal Limited Art Editions (ULAE) in a small Long Island studio where she hoped to publish illustrated books. Although she was not a print technician herself, she brought with her a lofty view of the potential of lithography. She encouraged and cajoled artists such as Larry Rivers, Jasper Johns and Robert Rauschenberg, who previously had had little interest or experience in printmaking, to draw on slabs of limestone. "I thought the second half of the twentieth century was no time to begin writing on rocks," was Rauschenberg's first reaction to lithography.[2] However, the artists' growing enthusiasm for what was to them an esoteric medium, finally matched hers. The exquisite and luxurious prints produced by these and other painters at ULAE over almost two decades exploited the extraordinary possibilities of the graphic medium.

At the same time that Tatyana Grosman was nursing her studio into existence, artist June Wayne acted on her concern that the craft of lithography in America was in a state of serious decline. In 1960, with a ten-year grant from the Ford Foundation, she started Tamarind Lithography Workshop in Los Angeles, where subsequently a great number of lithographers were trained. It was largely through the activities of these two workshops, ULAE and Tamarind, that printmaking assumed new significance in the American art world. A major result was the proliferation of Tamarind-inspired workshops throughout the country. An important offshoot was the emergence of the master printer, who assumed a level of importance equal to that of his peers in Europe.

Tyler's evolution as master printer coincides with the heightened awareness of printmaking in this country. It was at the Tamarind Lithography Workshop in his capacity as technical director that he totally immersed himself in various printmaking techniques. He came to Tamarind after attending art school and working in a variety of jobs, all of which were industry-related. Tyler decided in 1962 to resume his art studies; living in Indianapolis at the time, he enrolled at the Herron School of Art. There, he studied lithography under Garo Antreasian, who from 1960 to 1961 had been the first technical director of the Tamarind Lithography Workshop.

Although a career as a master printer was not foremost in his mind, Tyler left Indianapolis in 1963 to follow in Antreasian's footsteps as Tamarind's technical director. It was there that Tyler's love of technical processes took precedence over his work as an artist. He became so

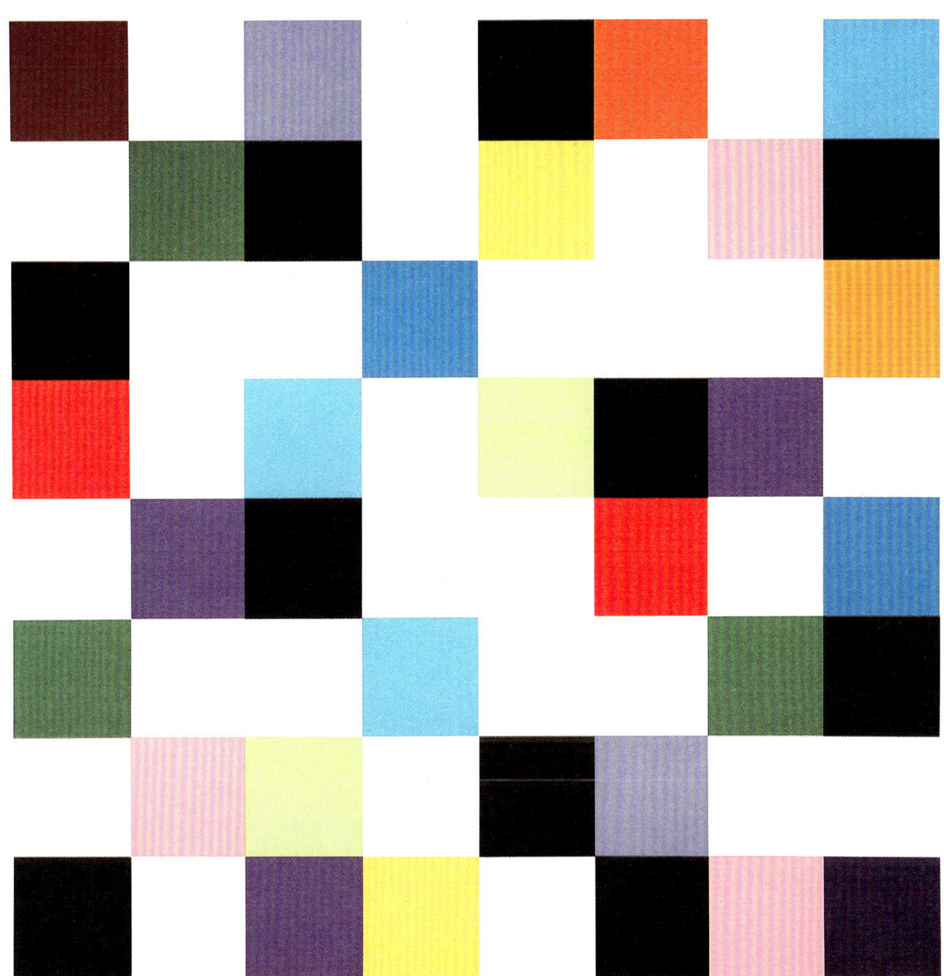

fascinated with his work in the print shop that it eventually superseded his studio painting. In 1965, Tyler left Tamarind to begin Gemini Ltd., whose objective was to attract leading artists to use its facilities in creating special print editions. A year later, in collaboration with two collectors of contemporary art, Sidney Felsen, the owner of an accounting firm, and Stanley Grinstein, a manufacturer, he founded Gemini G.E.L. The elegant, flawless surfaces of Gemini's first series of lithographs, Josef Albers's *White Line Squares* (1966), established a level of technical perfection that remains a hallmark of the celebrated workshop. Tyler's enthusiasm for the use of advanced industrial techniques in printmaking and his ability to work with a variety of strong-minded artists further distinguished the Gemini studio.

As printmaking workshops became part of the broader artistic landscape in America during the 1960s, more and more leading painters and sculptors tried their hand at it, often with astonishing results. David Hockney, Jasper Johns, Ellsworth Kelly, Roy Lichtenstein, Robert Motherwell, Claes Oldenburg, Robert Rauschenberg and Frank Stella all collaborated with Tyler and other printers at Gemini, translating their drawing and painting ideas, with increasing precision, into prints. The field was still very young and, as Tyler observes, craftsmen were still scrambling to enlarge and perfect their technical abilities as printmakers. To successfully reproduce the painted image in print, he says, was considered a desirable feat of technical virtuosity.[3]

It was about the same time that Gemini was attracting widespread admiration for the quality of its prints that Tyler became restless with his work there and began thinking about other directions to pursue, and in 1973 he left Los Angeles to establish his own print shop in rural Bedford Village, New York—a few minutes away from his friend Robert Motherwell and within easy commuting distance of New York City. Housed in an 1850 colonial-style carriage house, Tyler Graphics Ltd. was conceived from the outset as a workshop offering artists the full range of print media: etching, lithography, silkscreen, letterpress and monotype printing were all accommodated along with facilities for papermaking. Although some of the same artists with whom he worked at Gemini now come to Bedford Village, their prints reflect new attitudes toward the medium. In contrast to what Tyler describes as the pristine surfaces of earlier work, their new prints have a more varied surface character, reflecting the multiplicity of techniques available at Tyler Graphics. Editions are often small and some prints are created as unique variant impressions, often with hand-coloring by the artist. Indeed, many works produced in Bedford are one-of-a-kind.

Tyler has consistently encouraged artists to try new techniques and materials and such experiments have often been carried to heady limits. When David Hockney dropped by to have dinner with the printer in August 1978, so intrigued was he by the workshop's new experiments with paper pulp that he extended his visit into a forty-five day stay, working closely with Tyler and papermaker Lindsay Green. This intense session represented an unprecedented period of time for Tyler to devote to a single project, but, since then, he has embarked on a number of other technically innovative, complex projects that have required enormous outlays of his time as collaborator.

1. Judith Goldman, *American Prints: Process and Proofs,* New York: Whitney Museum of American Art, 1981, p. 17.
2. Ibid., p. 57.
3. Author's interview with Kenneth Tyler, March 30, 1984.

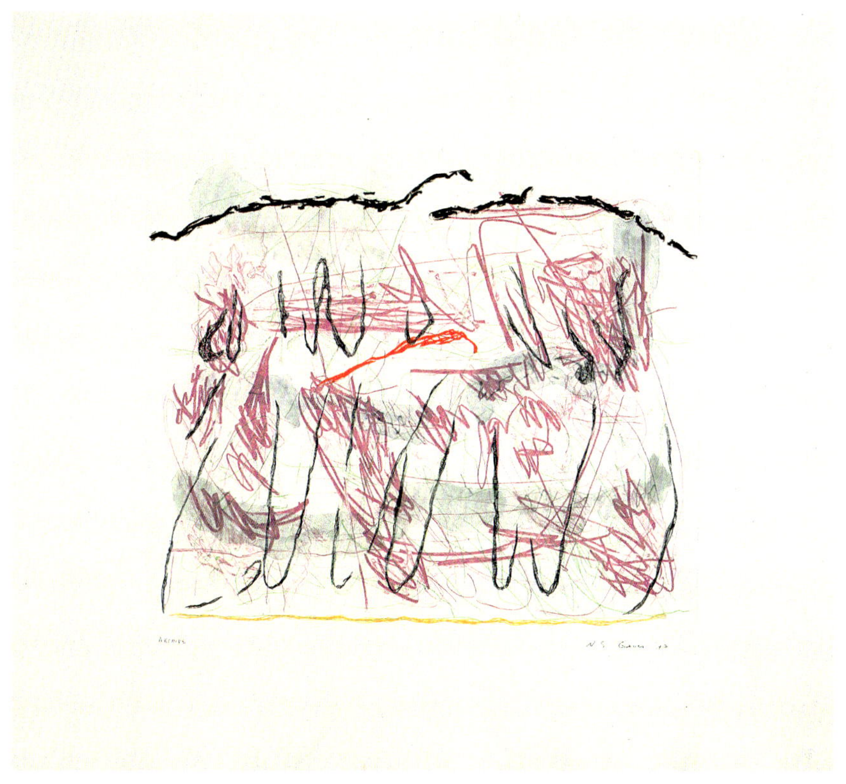

The artists working at Tyler Graphics over the past decade have produced a remarkably diverse body of work. When, in 1982, the British sculptor Anthony Caro came to Bedford to make prints, he ended up creating one hundred twenty-three, three-dimensional paperworks. Nancy Graves, on the other hand, whose subjects are drawn from skeletal forms, cave painting and weather patterns, fully exploited the range of techniques available—combining etching, aquatint, engraving and lithography with hand-coloring. The very nature of Alan Shields's imagery, with its heavily textured, brightly colored collage shapes, posed a special challenge to Tyler, who responded enthusiastically. With Tyler's help, Shields's idiosyncratic prints were constructed using multiple layers of handmade, lattice-work paper that is crushed, collaged and stitched together.

Indeed, if a single quality describes the widely diverse prints issued by Tyler Graphics, it is their distinctive surfaces. The textures of handmade papers, the saturated color that can be achieved by dyeing paper pulp, the scratching, incising and embossing, the surfeit of printers' ink furiously layered onto the prints, blur the usual distinctions between prints and work in other media. Tyler's objective, he says, is to help "free the medium" from its academic past and make it an ever greater vehicle for personal expression. The sophisticated facilities at Tyler Graphics that encourage artists to experiment have contributed to the transformation of the medium, giving it a radically new vocabulary.

Nancy Graves
*Ruis* 1977
etching, aquatint, engraving and solidified oil paint stick on Arches Cover mouldmade paper
31½ x 35½ edition 33

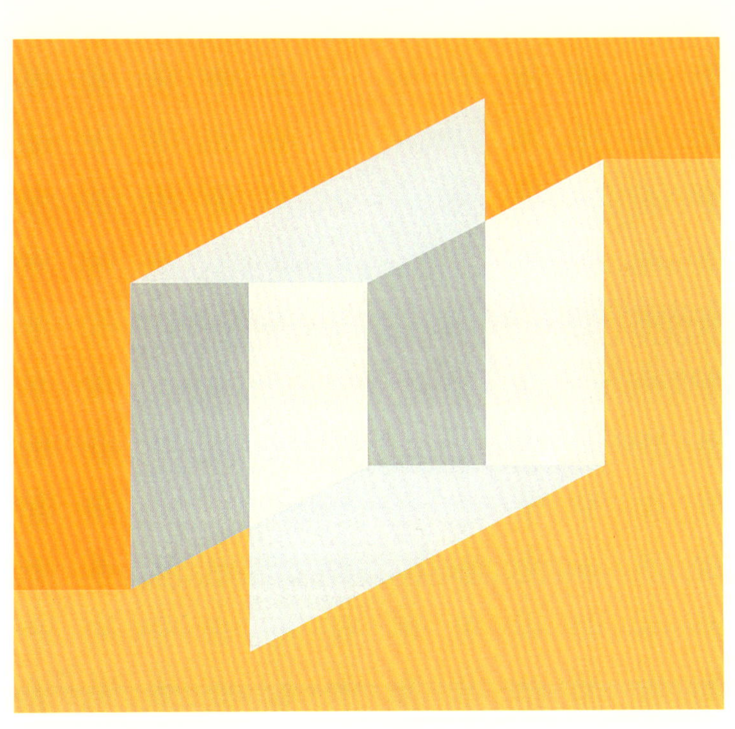

# Tyler Graphics: Range of Vision

*Elizabeth Armstrong*

The first two artists who made prints at Tyler Graphics Ltd. in 1974, Josef Albers and Robert Motherwell, were proponents of contrasting aesthetic philosophies. Albers's precise geometry characterized his printmaking as well as his painting. Motherwell's imagery, on the other hand, consisted of expressive, gestural shapes. In 1974, Tyler Graphics published Albers's *Gray Instrumentation I,* a portfolio of twelve screenprints distinguished by the interaction of meticulously defined blue-gray areas and precise registration of geometric forms. In contrast to Albers's severely controlled color and line, Motherwell's imagery, in his first Tyler print *The Stoneness of the Stone* (1974), is spontaneous almost to the point of abandon. He approached printmaking as a true Abstract Expressionist for whom the record of the journey was as important as the final image. By couching onto a larger sheet a small gray sheet of paper simulating the Bavarian limestone upon which the image was drawn, the outline of the stone became part of the design. In this sense, the print symbolized the essence of the lithographic process. Tyler's choice of these artists was prophetic. Subsequent production from his workshop has continued to range from the most rarified purism to intuitive expressionism.

Frank Stella, who has worked extensively with Ken Tyler since 1975, has managed to travel the stylistic spectrum defined by Albers and Motherwell. Several figurative artists, including David Hockney and Malcolm Morley, have also made prints at Tyler Graphics in which they have explored the range of traditional printmaking media as well as state-of-the-art technologies, often developing innovative hybrid forms.

Ken Tyler first met Josef Albers in 1963 when the distinguished artist was already 75 years old. Once a member of the Bauhaus movement in Weimar, Germany, Albers throughout his life pursued order and harmony in his art. While a visiting artist at Tamarind Lithography Workshop in Los Angeles, Albers became acquainted with Tyler and found in the younger man's printing a technical precision that paralleled his own formal interests. He later gave Tyler the authorization to make a series of prints based on one of his drawings; so pleased was he by the outcome that he asked Tyler to be his exclusive lithography printer. This experience was especially catalytic to Tyler's career because, at that moment, he says, Albers ". . . started me in print publishing. For the first time printmaking was hygienic, clean, pure and technically sound. There was, I think, no stopping me from that moment on."[4]

During the first four years at Tyler Graphics, four Albers portfolios were issued: *Gray Instrumentation I, Gray Instrumentation II, Mitered*

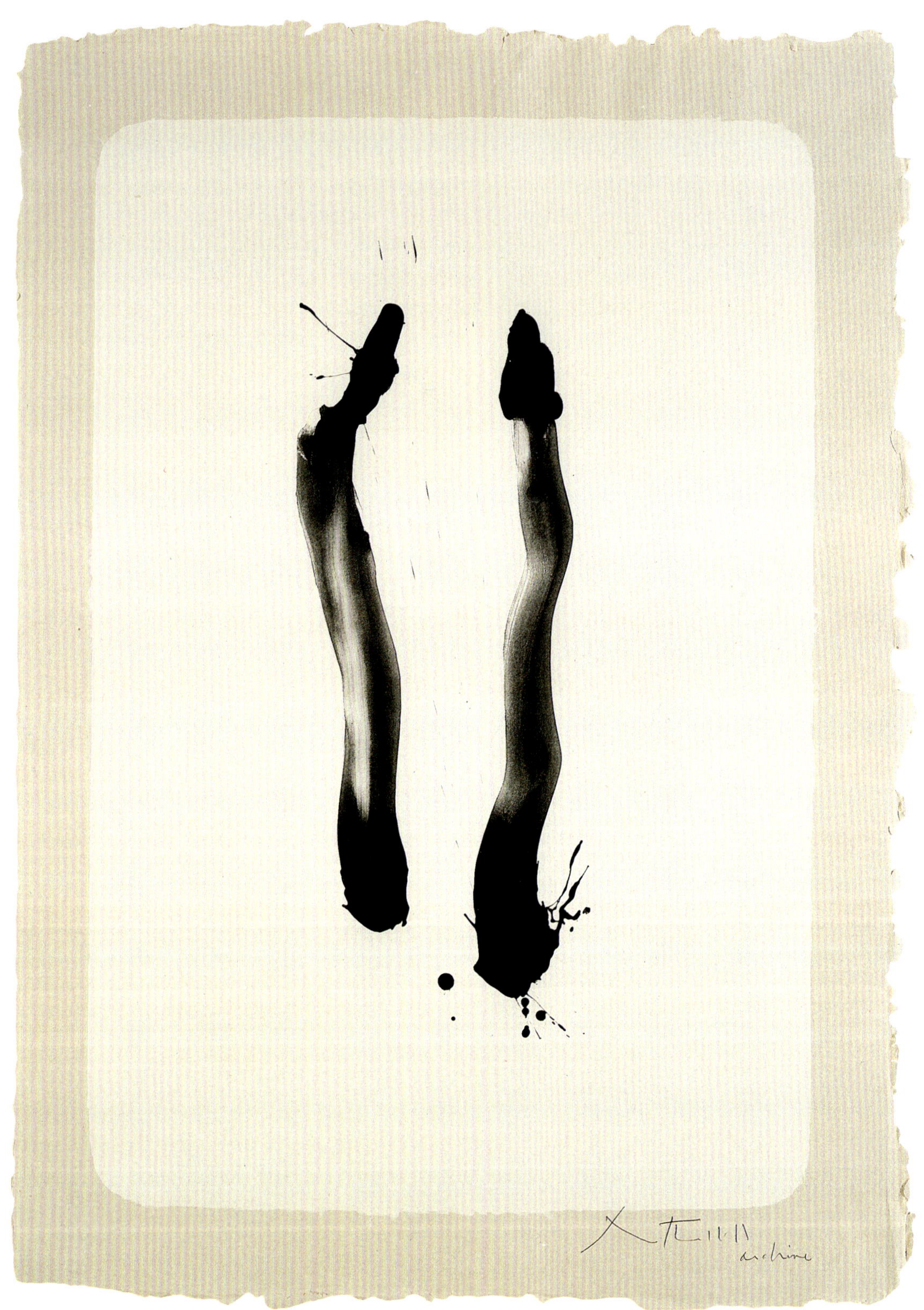

(p. 12)
Josef Albers
*Never Before d* 1975
screenprint on Arches 88 mouldmade paper
19 x 20 edition 46

Robert Motherwell
*The Stoneness of the Stone* 1974
lithograph on Twinrocker handmade laminated paper
41 x 30 edition 75

*Squares* and *Never Before*. The last series clearly shows one of Albers's primary intentions: to have the same colors interact in such a way that they look different from print to print, with corresponding variations in mood. The proofing process for these prints was extensive; Albers and Tyler pulled hundreds of impressions, experimenting with lithography plates, letterpress, zinc and magnesium cuts—even with woodcuts—before deciding to print the series with silkscreen. Tyler then made cutouts in numerous sample inks of different sections of the five-color scheme based on Albers's impromptu descriptions of colors that interested him, such as "spring green" and "honey yellow." Next, Albers, in his deliberate fashion, juxtaposed these cutouts, making over one hundred collages before arriving at his final twelve solutions.

Like Albers, a number of artists with whom Tyler has worked over the years have devoted themselves to exploring the expressive possibilities of geometric abstraction, among them Jack Tworkov, Ronald Davis, Frank Stella, Ellsworth Kelly and Kenneth Noland. In a 1981 print by Tworkov, *KTL #1*, four planar shapes—not quite rectangles or parallelograms—form a star-like configuration, floating in indeterminate space. In his 1975 etching, *Arch*, the young Californian Ron Davis also deals with spatial ambiguity using folded planes caught in a web of perspectival lines, creating the illusion of deep space. The painterly, stained background of the print was achieved through a special process developed by Tyler using dyes and pigmented paper pulp. These early experiments with color-impregnated pulp reflected Tyler's fascination with the inherent qualities of paper that has grown into what amounts to a paper pulp mania at Tyler Graphics.

Frank Stella was among the first to utilize pulp in a sequence of reliefs. Though he and Tyler had made prints together since 1967, in what had been his minimal geometric style, this project marked a dramatic departure from their earlier efforts. These 1975 paperworks were based on Stella's first paintings to employ relief elements, the *Polish Village* series of 1970–73.[5] As are the paintings, these are strongly reminiscent of earlier twentieth-century Russian Constructivism, particularly Kasimir Malevich's architectural drawings and Vladimir Tatlin's painted reliefs in which strong kinetic forces are contained within the strong geometry of the forms. Molded into angular, geometric motifs, the paper pulp was then hand-colored by Stella in a range of brilliant colors. Like his striped canvases of the 1960s, these were "shaped" constructions whose irregular external outlines were defined by the geometric shapes within.

Tyler has delighted in introducing one artist after another to the wonders of paper pulp. Even Ellsworth Kelly, long regarded as the ultimate purist for whom hard-edged geometry in clear spectrum color was the only answer, found himself beguiled by the process. He was intrigued by this new, malleable material, and in it saw great possibilities for fusing color and surface; the technique had a decided influence on Kelly's imagery. As he overlaid and fused layers of pulp to build a surface, his characteristic hard edges were obliterated and as the color bled from one shape to another his geometry took on a fluid, ambiguous quality. In *Colored Paper Images* (1976), Kelly's usually precise shapes were further softened by the introduction of gray tones and the spongy surface of the pulp that greedily absorbs and dilutes the bright ink colors that permeate it.

Kenneth Noland, whose stained canvas paintings of the 1950s helped introduce a new aesthetic in American abstract art, was an ideal candidate for paper pulp exploration. The fast, spontaneous process of working with color-dyed paper felt as familiar to Noland as applying wide bands and circles to unprimed canvas, thereby making the paint an integral part of the surface. In his 1978 *Handmade Papers*, Noland, with great facility and inventiveness, used this same principle of color-impregnated surface.

Although working with paper pulp has close analogies to painting and even to sculpture, making prints by more traditional means requires an analytical approach that is often at odds with the way many artists work. For example, the Abstract Expressionist painters felt particularly hampered by the constraints the print studio placed on spontaneity and size. Their concerns with textural surface, density of color and large scale were at odds with the compulsive processes demanded by the craft. Impatient with the methodology of traditional printmaking, they preferred the immediate results of their heroic confrontations with canvas. Robert Motherwell, the only New York School painter to have worked extensively in graphics, recalls his entry into printmaking as an uneasy one, much like " . . . what Alice must have felt when catapulted into Wonderland."[6] Today, even as one of America's most prolific printmakers, Motherwell maintains a naiveté about printmaking techniques and entrusts them to the medium's most talented masters. In that spirit he has established a close working relationship with Tyler. Since 1974 Motherwell has been especially prolific, creating images that run the emotional gamut from delicate lyricism to explosive violence.

Motherwell constantly utilizes certain basic themes with which he has become identified. Prominent among these is the sensual Spanish Elegy motif, a cluster of rectangular and ovoid forms that first gained prominence during the 1950s in a sequence of paintings whose theme was the tragedy of the Spanish Civil War. This percussive symbol—a fusion of organic and geometric elements—is not limited to his painting, but takes on a fierce new vitality in the graphic medium. In the heroically scaled *Lament for Lorca*, a 1982 lithograph, the forms so fill the space that they seem about to explode. Motherwell has invested this predominantly black image with a variety of matte and glossy surfaces—the result of four aluminum plate printings over a black wash printed from limestone—to the point where the lithograph is a brooding, somber mass. Because his art is so calligraphic, so dependent upon rich, eloquent strokes, one is always conscious of the act of drawing and painting; the gesture is as much the essence of his prints as of his monumental painted allegories.

The Abstract Expressionists' search for symbols that would fuse emotion and form was maintained by a "second generation" of artists, among them Helen Frankenthaler and Joan Mitchell. In the early 1950s, Frankenthaler developed a "soak-stain" technique in which she was able to eliminate both line and surface texture as elements in painting, thereby emphasizing color and form as subject in a way similar to that used by Kenneth Noland and Morris Louis in their stained canvases.

Frankenthaler has made prints at Tyler Graphics since 1976; in 1977, she created the first woodblock print to be produced at Tyler Graphics, *Essence Mulberry*. While Frankenthaler had made several woodcuts before, she still found it the most challenging technique to use. For example, instead of dark marks on a light surface, each slice into the woodblock creates a blank line and the uncut portions a solid mass. Multi-colored prints require a separate block for each color, further complicating the image developing process. Yet, if Frankenthaler finds the process daunting, she has obtained outstanding results in woodcut. The fluid shapes and lush colors of her block surfaces have given new vitality to this venerable technique.

Joan Mitchell's kinetic gestural style, so evident in her large-scale abstract landscape paintings, was admirably translated into prints when she began working with Tyler in 1981. As in her paintings, these prints have densely packed surfaces of scratchy marks and rough color planes, indications of generalized forms in nature. Indeed, light, color, rhythm and space—as opposed to descriptive shapes—are the dominant subject matter of her prints. The loaded brushstrokes of her paintings have their parallel in the flowing quality of lines and the raw textured marks of the lithographic crayon. Mitchell's frenetic skeins in the 1981 lithograph *Bedford II* completely fill and energize the picture plane.

Nancy Graves's work represents a decidedly different form from Mitchell's which, in true Abstract Expressionist fashion, derives from a wholly intuitive means of image building. Graves's art, though also richly detailed, is a highly subjective reaction to abstract patterns found in the rational world, such as topographic maps and weather photographs. She is a gatherer of scientific information which she transmits through her idiosyncratic system into vibrant dot and line codes that create a complicated play of figure and ground. Her first prints at Tyler Graphics in 1977, in which a cheerful randomness of form prevails, are reminiscent of her paintings of that period that explore the speed and duration of gesture. Independent of topographic or other descriptive sources, color and line are used expressively in these elaborate prints that combine etching with aquatint, drypoint and engraving—finally to be hand-colored by the artist with pastel and oil stick. In her recent prints made with Tyler in 1981, Graves incorporates shapes and patterns found in her sculpture. In *Calibrate*, for example, skeletal forms refer back to the camels and camel bones of her earliest sculptures of the late 1960s.

A number of contemporary sculptors have been drawn to the print medium. Anthony Caro chose to work with handmade paper spatially, twisting and folding the rough textured material into various relief-like configurations. Both Kelly and Stella used Tyler Graphics resources to develop some of their ideas into three-dimensional objects and both were, of course, especially sensitive to the malleable character of paper pulp. By contrast, other sculptors have preferred to translate their primal images into strong linear drawings. The gestural lithographs of Mark di Suvero, for example, are directly related to his large-scale wood and metal sculptures and these graphic images suggest studies for richly heroic pieces.

For Michael Heizer, whose monumental earth sculptures in the deserts of Nevada and California sprawl over vast land areas,

David Hockney
*Midnight Pool* (Paper Pool 19)
1978
colored and pressed paper pulp
$81\frac{1}{2}$ x $92\frac{1}{2}$ edition unique

printmaking has become a particularly significant medium. It has been a means of dealing with geometry in an elegantly calibrated manner, and on a human scale distinct from his enormous sculptures. His first series of Tyler prints, *Circles I-IV* (1976), reflects Heizer's interest in the interplay of simple geometric forms as this occurs in his earthworks and sculptures. In *Circles I-III*, he methodically divided an intaglio plate circle into eight segments and then manipulated their color and placement to set up a series of relationships. *Circle IV* is animated by abstract markings that convey a similar sense of fragmentation. Heizer's series of multi-media prints and monotypes made in 1983, with their complex interplay of architectonic forms, animated markings and verbal notations, reflect a considerably more spontaneous approach to the medium. Sculptural elements are presented again in different relationships, but they co-exist with layers of colorful markings. These include scrawled words and numbers that direct the viewer to the artist's working process.

The great draftsman, Claes Oldenburg, makes numerous sketches, many of which foreshadow his sculptures. His proposals for fantastic monuments are drawn with extraordinary old-masterish facility, and he chose to make use of traditional lithography in his Tyler print, *Chicago Stuffed With Numbers* (1977). A favorite Oldenburg theme, the "soft" city map—in this case Chicago—is capriciously filled with numbers drawn as pudgy, pillow-like shapes, evocative of the artist's soft sculptures.

In his architectural motifs, Roy Lichtenstein took advantage of Ken Tyler's interest in using industrial techniques, and the *Entablatures,* which emerged after a sixteen-month collaboration, combine silkscreen, lithography and collaged metallic foil elements with deep embossing. A variety of machined, cast and etched metal parts were custom-made for the embossing dies which simulated the bas-relief images in the series. While these works are based on actual architectural fragments, their hard edges, clean lines, optical patterns and gleaming surfaces place emphasis on their highly abstract character.

Tyler has enjoyed working with a number of other artists identified in some measure with Pop and Pop-related developments here and in England, and among the latter have been Richard Hamilton, Malcolm Morley and David Hockney. Hockney's collaboration with Tyler has been a particularly long and prolific one, beginning at Gemini Ltd. in Los Angeles. Hockney's lithograph and silkscreen portrait of Tyler called the *The Master Printer of Los Angeles* (1973) commemorates their early association. Since then, Hockney's approach to printmaking has broadened considerably, ranging from elegant descriptive drawings of such favorite models as Celia and Gregory as well as still lifes and California landscapes to extremely innovative projects such as the monumental paper pools. This series was initiated with Tyler in 1977 shortly after Hockney had finished designing the sets and costumes for *The Magic Flute* at the Glyndebourne Festival Opera. The simple planar images of Egyptian architecture, which he incorporated into the opera design, find their equivalents in this dazzling series. Having been introduced by Tyler to the mysteries and pleasures of paper pulp, Hockney used this material to create large color-saturated images that

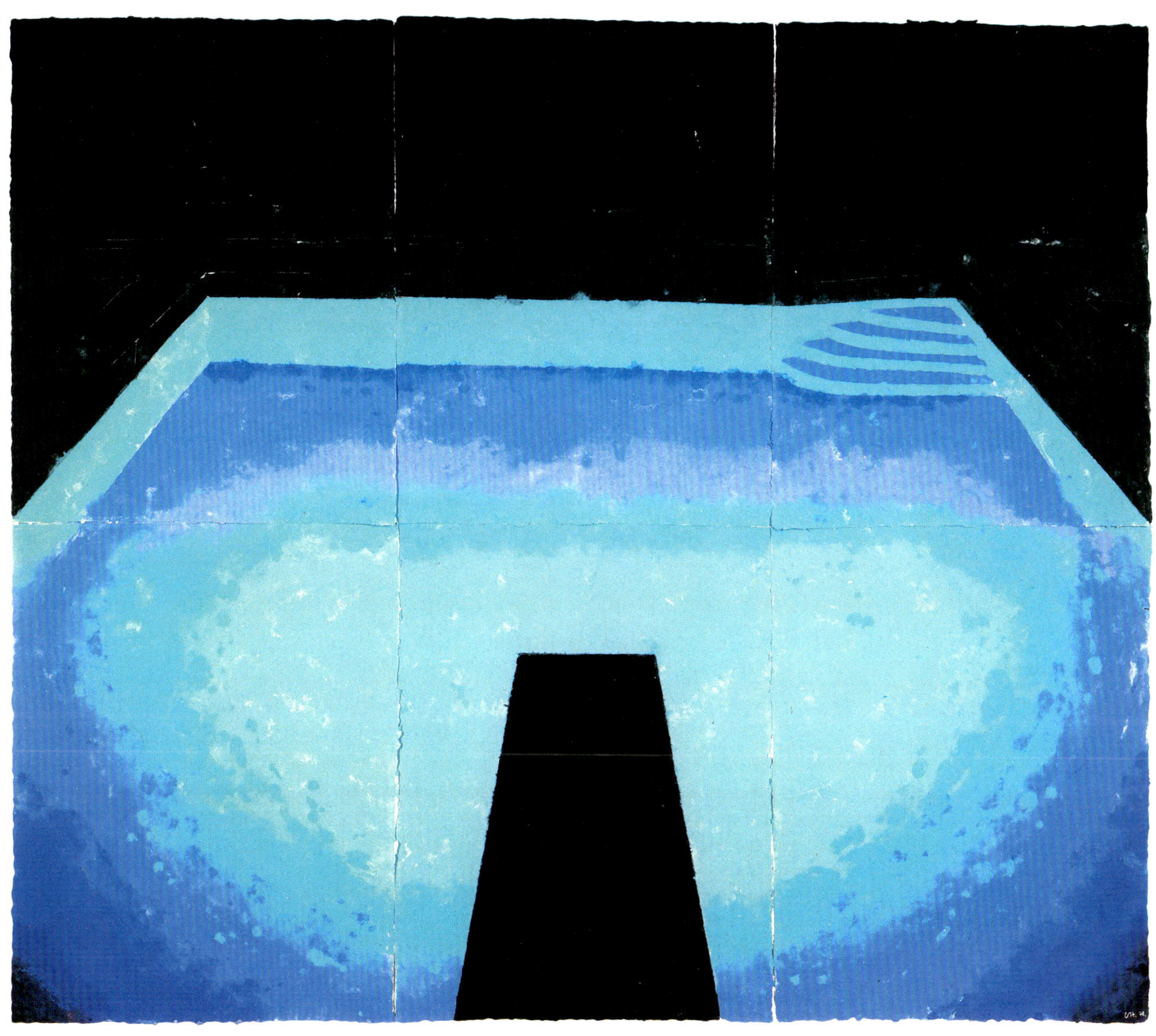

capture the radiance, density and reflectivity of water. In these paper pools, the English artist abandoned his characteristic linear technique in favor of large color masses that virtually bleed into one another at their edges. At the same time, Hockney began work on twenty-five color lithographs, again using the pool theme. In these freely drawn impressions, all forms are subordinated to the decorative quality of the design. Squiggly lines and washes that represent light on water are evoked in Hockney's facile handling of the tusche medium. Here, water, a subject prevalent in Hockney's work since the 1960s, is treated in an abstract manner that is frequently reminiscent of Japanese woodblock prints.

The flat color and depthless quality of the Japanese print is also suggested in the boldly decorative work of Ed Baynard, whose formally composed floral still lifes, made with Tyler in 1980, were clearly inspired by the classical techniques of the Ukiyo-e woodblock artists. By incorporating patterned woodgrain and using both hand-wiped and brayer-inked blocks, Baynard arrived at a delicate balance between description and abstraction in these clear, elemental images that belie the complexity of the process that produced them. *The Print Scarf*, for example, was printed in twenty-nine colors that required fourteen woodblocks.

At the other end of the spectrum are Frank Stella's technically hybrid prints that, as a result of lengthy experiments in Tyler's workshop, have grown increasingly complex in imagery. Stella's prints as well as paintings have undergone a remarkable transformation, to the point where he has singlemindedly reinvigorated pure abstraction with a new infusion of expressionistic ardor.

The *Exotic Birds* paintings and prints signaled the transition in Stella's work. While his iconography continued to be based on drafting room tools, French curves now dominated protractors, and these motifs, which imply the plumage of exotic birds, were laid down with careening exuberance. Lurid colors, crayon scribbles and glitzy metallic sprinkles were further embellishments to these flashy prints. The *Exotic Birds* were followed by the *Circuits*, a series of prints with increasingly frenetic imagery and "loaded" surfaces. Stella used the residue from an earlier project as the basis for these prints: the patterns left by laser beams on the wood backings used to cut the metal forms for his 1981 series of painted constructions also titled *Circuits*. Stella was so fascinated by the serpentine lines of the tracings that he had them transferred to relief blocks. Tyler evolved a method of working with Stella on these prints that entailed, among other things, multi-colored handmade paper, etching, line-cut, woodcut, screenprinting and hand-wiping with stencil printing. With their writhing overload of lines, tones and textures, the *Circuits* prints (named for auto racing tracks that Stella visited in the late 1970s) such as *Imola Five II*, which combines intaglio and relief printing, and *Talladega Three II*, which mixes the range of techniques, personify Stella's most energetic and inventive side.

Tyler's non-traditional approach to printmaking continues to attract artists whose attitude toward the medium is equally open. In the past, Alan Shields was put off by the technical aspects of the process and by what he regarded as the lack of personality associated with most printmaking. While working at Tyler Graphics, however, he found the situation anything but mechanical; he had ample opportunity to try new things. Few print shops would be willing to take the risks of working with an artist for whom the exploration of process and materials had become such a complicated ritual. Shields's demands on the print shop equalled those he made on himself. His series of prints, *The Castle Window Set* (1981) evolved over a year-long period of collaboration with printers at Tyler Graphics during which he experimented with handmade paper, etching, aquatint and relief printing from wood, magnesium and linoleum plates—even sewing directly onto these prints. Since his first Tyler prints made in 1978, he has made over thirty editions in which he has continued to experiment. In his hands, paper underwent startling metamorphoses. He perforated, ripped, layered and soaked it with pigment to create fantastic microcosms suggesting everything from out-of-control yeast molds to kaleidoscopic visions of the universe.

The English artist Richard Smith began his career in London's lively Pop scene during the 1960s, yet he was never interested in subject matter from popular culture. His search has been for new ways to deal with form and color in three-dimensional planar shapes. He went through the shaped canvas syndrome and by the mid-1970s was making kite-like constructions of paper and cloth. Tyler's enthusiasm for the possibilities of paper pulp soon had an eager new convert. The material was ideally suited to Smith's interests and formal vocabulary. In his *Cartouche* series, made in 1980, he and Tyler came up with the idea of laminating paper pulp to both sides of dyed cotton fabric. Constructed from two or three rectangular panels that overlap when hung on a wall, each *Cartouche* wall hanging is unique in form, color and size.

A recent visitor to Tyler Graphics was the Minnesota artist Steven Sorman. Prior to his new association with Tyler, he had distinguished himself as an accomplished printmaker in a variety of techniques, often utilizing layers of papers and fabrics to create delicately textured, seemingly weightless images. However, instead of encouraging Sorman to continue to refine his printmaking skills, Tyler suggested that the young artist take a different tack; he urged him to try working solely in monotype. The results are startling—large, spontaneously conceived prints that are filled with paradoxical episodes: delicate linear configurations combined with raw, slashing brushstrokes; smooth and elegant shapes juxtaposed with harsh, gritty ones. In contrast to his usually discreet eloquence, these bold prints mark a vivid new direction for Sorman.

Among contemporary master printers, Kenneth Tyler is regarded as the most assertive in his working relationships with artists. He is as challenged by their aspirations as they are by his. "What always excites me most is the one that is just about to happen tomorrow. It's just a little bit out of reach."[7] Tyler continually finds himself thinking about that next project, tantalized by the possibility of discovery.

4. Kenneth Tyler, quoted by J. Goldman in "The Master Printer of Bedford, New York," *Artnews*, September 1977, p. 53.
5. Richard Axsom, *The Prints of Frank Stella, A Catalogue Raisonné 1967–82*, New York: Hudson Hills Press in association with the University of Michigan Museum of Art, Ann Arbor, 1973, p. 178.
6. Robert Motherwell, quoted by Stephanie Terenzio, *The Painter and the Printer, Robert Motherwell's Graphics 1943–1980*, New York: American Federation of the Arts, 1980, p. 13.
7. Author's interview with Kenneth Tyler, March 30, 1984.

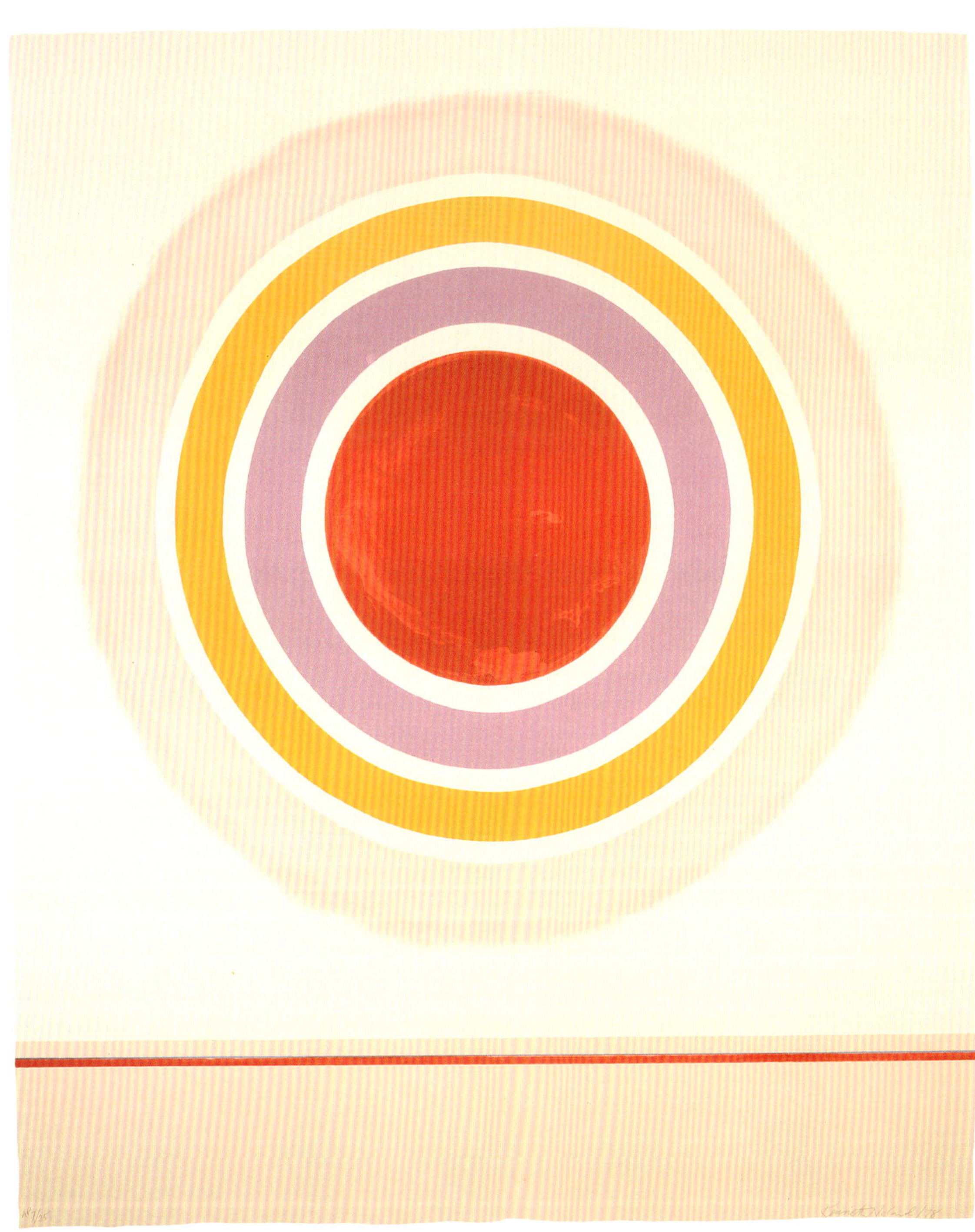

Kenneth Noland
*Blush* 1978
lithograph on Rives BFK
mouldmade paper
36 x 30 edition 50

Robert Motherwell
*Lament for Lorca* 1982
lithograph on TGL handmade
paper
44 x 61 edition 52

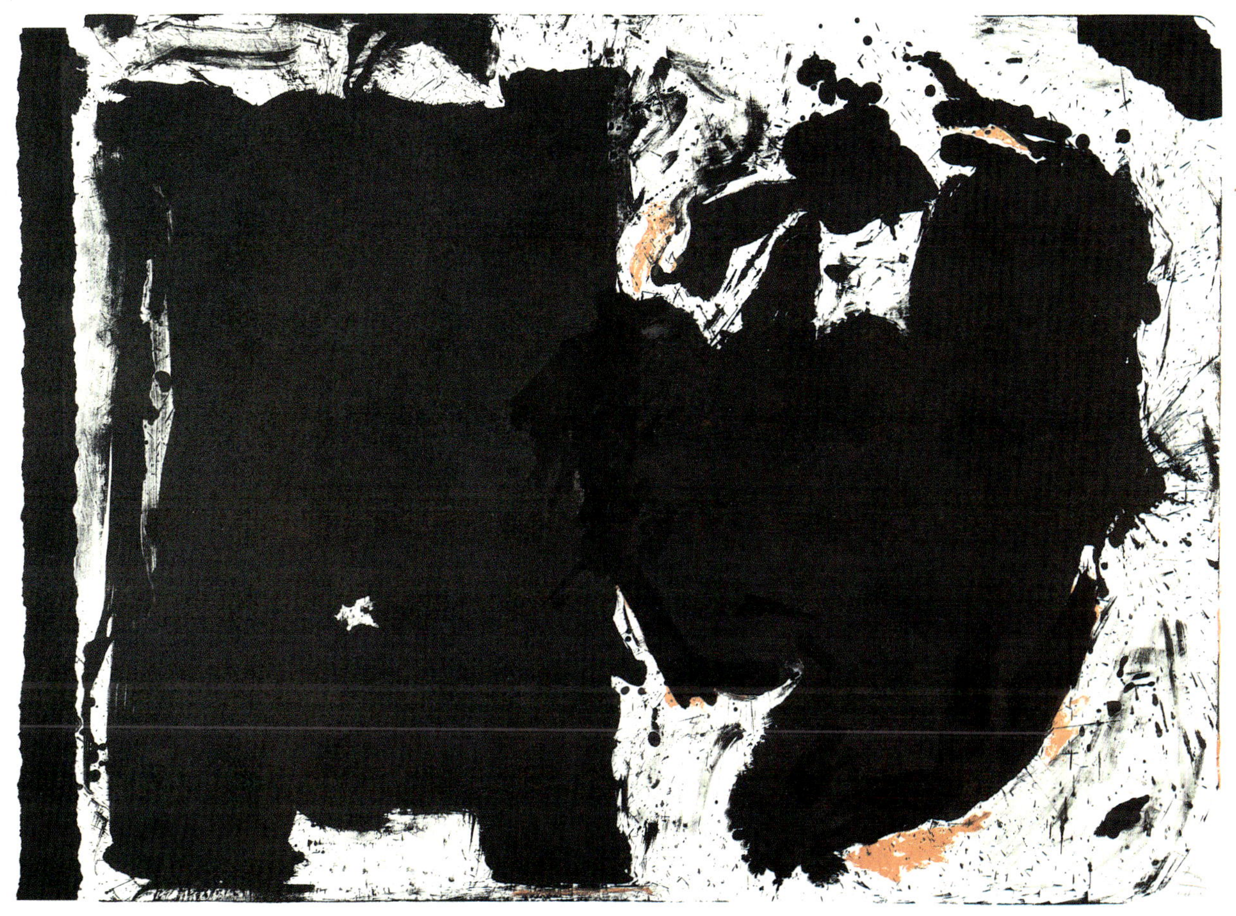

Ellsworth Kelly
*Colored Paper Image VII* 1976
colored paper pulp laminated to
TGL handmade paper
46½ x 32½ variant edition

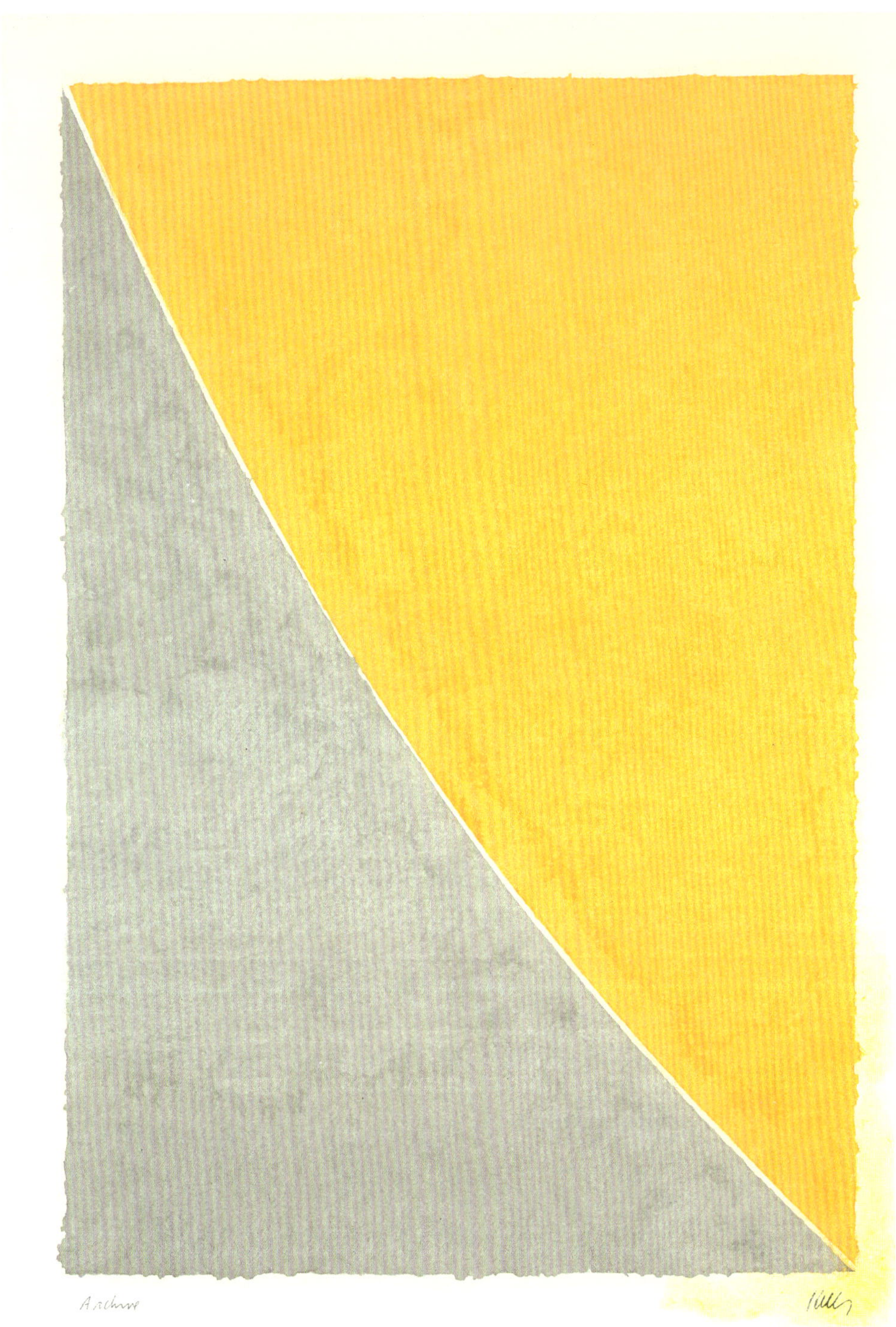

Frank Stella
*Talladega Three II* 1982
relief-printed etching on TGL
multi-colored handmade paper
66 x 51⅜ edition 30

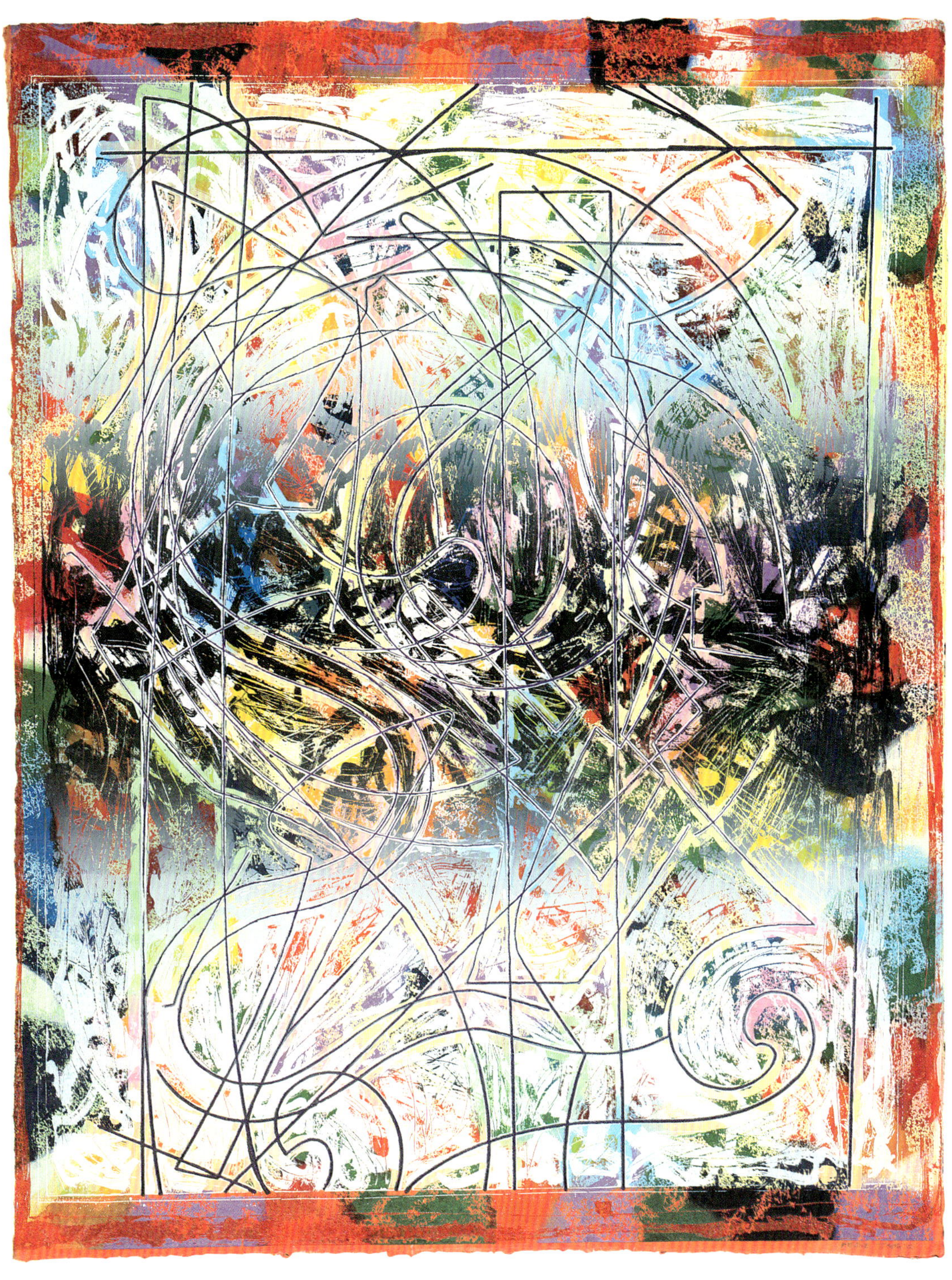

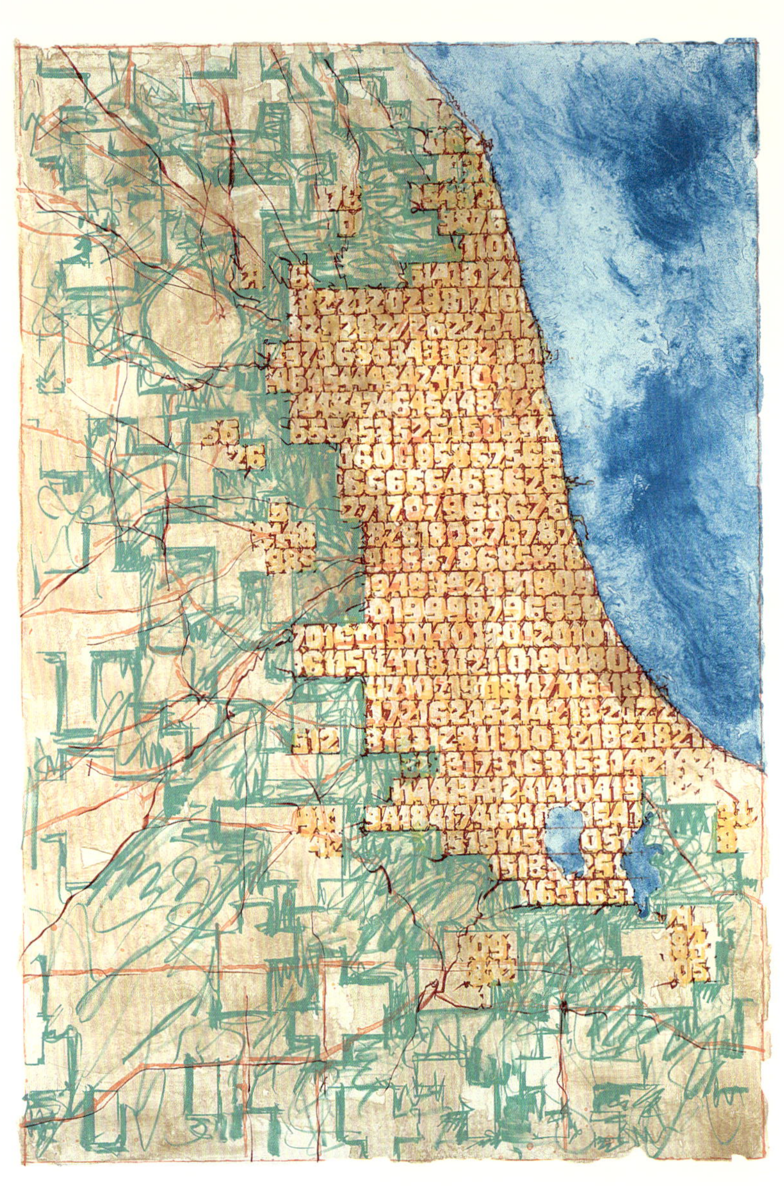

Claes Oldenburg
*Chicago Stuffed with Numbers*
1977
lithograph on Arches Cover mouldmade paper
47½ x 30½ edition 85

Roy Lichtenstein
*American Indian Theme VI* 1979
woodblock print on Japanese Suzuki paper
37½ x 50¼ edition 50

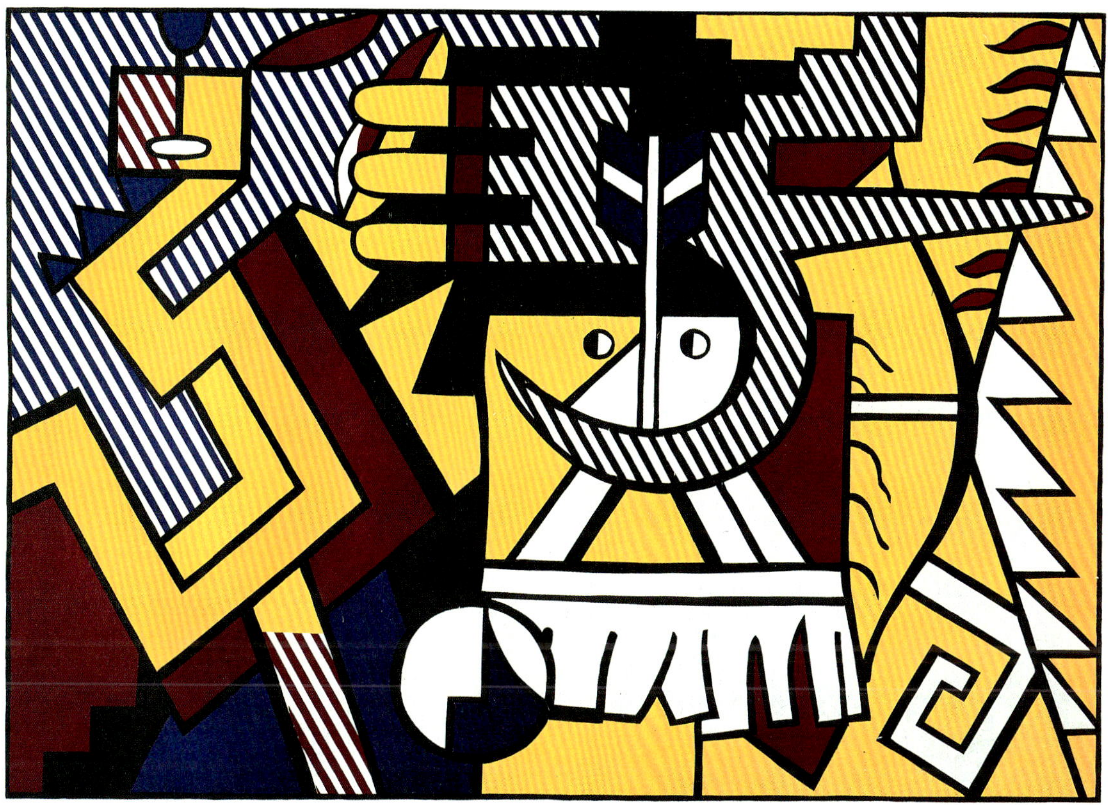

Michael Heizer
*45°, 90°, 180°* 1983
lithograph, screenprint, etching, rubber stamp on TGL handmade paper
32 x 46½ edition 40

Alan Shields
*Odd Job* 1984
etching, woodblock, relief print on TGL handmade paper
42 x 42 edition 46

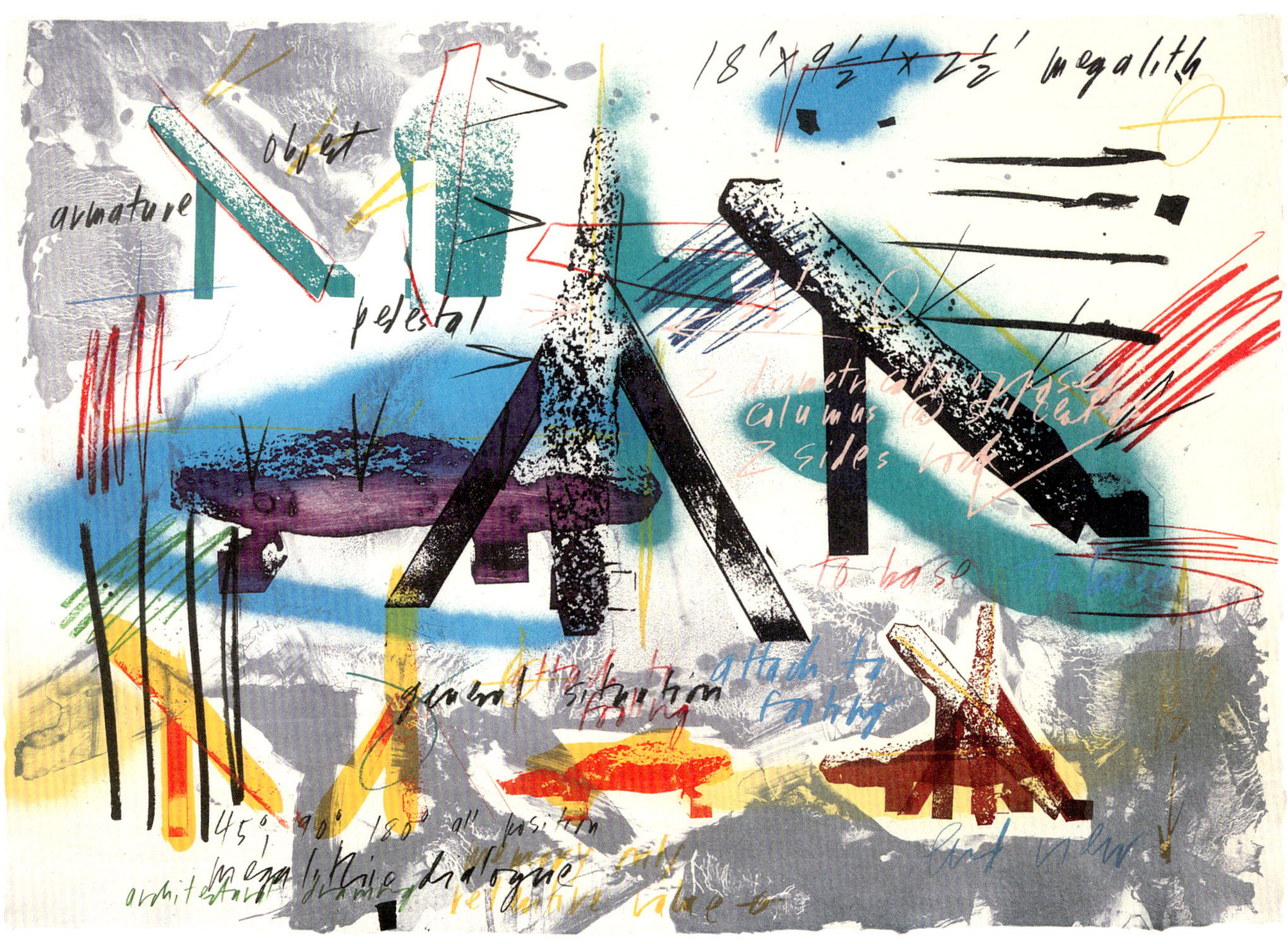

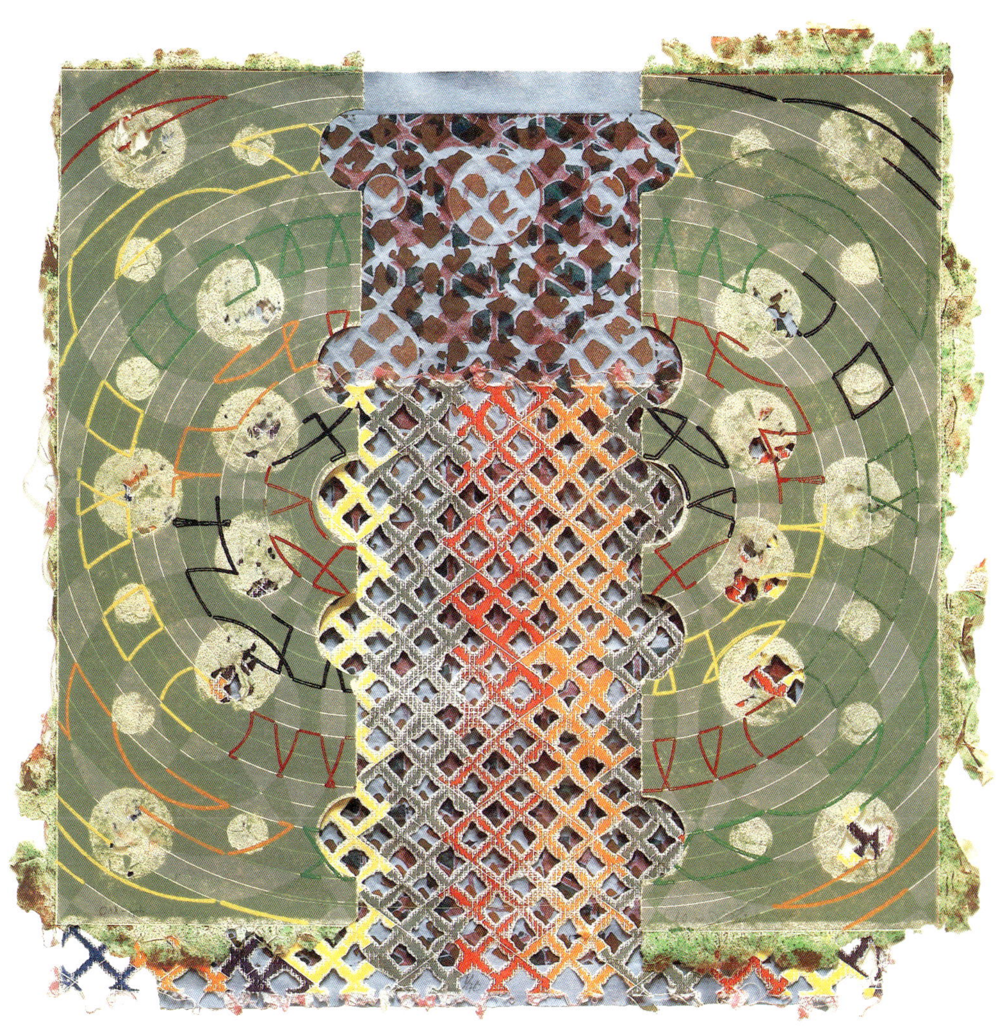

## Glossary

Note: This glossary is drawn largely from the *Paper and Printmaking Glossary* compiled and published by Leonard Schlosser and Kenneth Tyler in 1978.

**Aquatint**
A tonal method of intaglio printing achieved by adhering fine particles of acid-resistant material (powdered resin, spray lacquer or paint) to a plate. The aquatint is treated in the acid bath as an etching, producing a textured surface. This surface, when printed, produces even tones without gradation or blending. Aquatint is often used in combination with other intaglio techniques.

**Colored Paper**
In contemporary hand papermaking, many techniques, old and new, have been employed with traditional as well as with new forms of coloring either to color the pulp in the vat or to color the newly couched sheet of paper. This approach to color papermaking often results in the creation of one-of-a-kind papers. The following terms relate to this approach to handmade paper either in sheet form or as a three-dimensional object.

*Color pulp* A fiber mixture that has any type of coloring matter such as pigments, dyes, paints, colored rags, or a combination added to it to make color paper. Color pulps may be intermixed in the beater or in the vat or in small containers to make uniform or non-uniform colored paper.

*Embedding* Applying to the surface of a newly couched sheet of paper any material such as rags, threads, vegetation, etc. If placed in a press with the wet paper, the foreign material will be made more an integral part of the sheet, imparting the object's color and shape to the paper surface.

*Mixed pulp* The random effect of mixing two or more contrasting color pulps in the vat to create mottled color papers. Coloring pulp to permit certain fibers to accept color selectively produces a random colored pulp which results in paper having a veined look, historically termed "granite paper."

*Staining* The art of applying liquid colors to the surface of a newly couched sheet of paper. During pressing of the paper, the color matter may spread or bleed even further into the surface fibers of the newly made paper. Historically, the application of coloring material to the surface of dry paper.

**Couching**
Transferring the wet, newly-formed sheet of paper from the mold by pressure to a wet felt. Two or more newly-formed sheets may be couched one to another (of like or unlike size, color, character or thickness) in order to form a multi-layered sheet.

**Deckle edges**
The rough edges on handmade paper. Originally considered an imperfection, the deckle edge came back into fashion with the handcraft revival in the last decade of the 19th century.

**Drypoint**
An intaglio process wherein marks are made on a plate with a sharp, pointed instrument. This tool creates a ragged curl on the side(s) of the incised line. Both the incised line and the ragged burr receive ink when the plate is wiped with ink, giving a distinctive furry look to the line. Drypoint is usually done on copper plates and is often combined with other intaglio techniques such as etching and aquatint.

**Edition**
The total prints of a completed single image or series of images that are numbered and signed by the artist and not retained as proofs.

**Embossing**
The formation by pressure of a relief design in any material.

**Engraving**
An intaglio technique in which a metal plate is incised with a wedge-shaped tool called a burin or graver. The tool is pushed over the plate at an angle which permits the cutting action to go from a deep to a tapered stroke.

**Etching**
An intaglio technique in which the drawn marks are created in the metal plate by chemical rather than mechanical action. Either a hard-ground or soft-ground preparation is thinly applied to the plate's surface and dried. Using various tools the artist draws through the ground exposing the metal. The plate is then immersed in an acid bath which removes uniform layers of the exposed metal and produces recessed areas in the plate surface. Using stop-out varnishes, selected areas of exposed metal can be etched to different depths. Etching is often combined with other intaglio techniques.

**Impression**
A print taken by any method.

**Intaglio**
The generic name for aquatint, engraving, etching, mezzotint and drypoint. In these processes the elements that create the image are made up of recesses and indentations in the plate. Ink is then applied to the recessed areas of the printing plate by wiping, rolling and/or a combination of both. For this type of printing, the paper is dampened so that it will, under printing pressure, be squeezed into all the inked recesses of the plate.

**Line-cut**
A method of relief printing where the non-image areas are removed from the plate by such techniques as acid etching or cutting with tools.

**Lithography**
The planographic (flat-surfaced) printing process based upon the antipathy of grease and water. The printing elements used are stone and aluminum plates which are grained to varying degrees of roughness. Image areas can be created using pencils, crayons, tusche, various

grease, lacquer or synthetic materials, as well as photochemical and transfer processes. After the stone or plate is drawn, a treatment using a solution of gum arabic and nitric acid is applied over the total surface, chemically producing water-receptive (non-printing) areas and grease-receptive (image) areas. Once this procedure is carried out the stone or plate must always be stored with a dried layer of gum arabic over the total surface. During printing this gum film is washed off with water and the printing element kept continuously dampened with water so the hand roller, charged with oil base ink, can be rolled over the surface until the image (grease-receptive areas) is sufficiently charged with ink. When fully inked, paper is laid directly on top of the stone or plate and run through the press to print the image.

**Maquette**
A small preliminary model designed to gauge the general appearance or composition of the three-dimensional object that is planned.

**Mezzotint**
An intaglio method in which the surface of a metal plate is uniformly incised with a tool called a rocker. The technique of mezzotint creates patterns of tones on the polished plate. By scraping and burnishing, gradations from dark to light are produced. The mezzotint process often involves a combination of other intaglio methods.

**Mixed-media**
Prints made by a combination of techniques such as screenprint, lithography, embossing, casting or any method of duplication. Many of the methods used do not yield exactly repeatable images. Variations are created and controlled within the developed range of each technique by the artist and collaborator.

**Monotype**
A single printed image incapable of being reprinted identically. Painting an image on glass or other materials and printing it directly before the ink has dried is the most common form of monotype.

**Pochoir**
A process for making multicolor prints and coloring black and white prints using stencils and stencil brush.

**Printing element**
Any material, such as stone, metal plate, screen, etc., upon which a design is created for the purpose of making an impression. In prints involving more than one color, usually a separate printing element is drawn for each color. The exception is when one printing element has various colors (more than one, or as many as technically possible) applied to it and produces these colors on the paper in one impression pull from the press.

**Proof**
An impression taken at any stage in the making of a print that is not part of the edition.

*Artist's proof* Impressions outside the numbered edition made especially for the artist, usually marked as "Artist's Proofs" or "A.P."

*Trial proof* An impression taken in the process of creating an image, often incorporating new revisions to the plate or stone. Technical notations regarding the quality of printing or image are often written on the print by the artist, printer or both.

*Working proof* A proof on which the artist has drawn, painted or collaged, often used during proofing to indicate changes.

*Cancellation proof* An impression taken from a plate, often marked with an X to designate the end of an edition.

**Pulp**
The reduced fibers which have been diluted with water and are ready to be formed into sheets of paper. Also called "stuff" in the paper-making process.

**Relief printing**
A generic term used to describe techniques such as woodcut or line-cut. The printed impression is created by the raised areas of the image on the surface of the printing element. The recessed areas do not print, but during printing the paper is often pushed into these sunken areas creating an embossed effect on the impression.

**Screenprint**
A stencil technique using a fabric (silk or synthetic) stretched tightly over a frame where the non-printing areas on the fabric are blocked out by an adhering stencil. The image areas are open fabric through which ink or paint is forced with a tool called a squeegee. The screen frame is hinged onto a table (usually a vacuum table). The material to be printed is placed on the table, the screen placed on top, and with the squeegee ink is applied through the screen openings directly onto the paper. Unlike many of the other printing media, screenprinting can be done on nearly any material.

**State**
Every revision of a plate, block, or stone from which one or more impressions are pulled.

**Stenciling**
The general term for the process in which an image is cut from paper or cardboard so that when inked or painted the image can be repeated throughout the edition.

**Wiping**
The process of removing ink from the unbitten surface of an intaglio plate, leaving ink only in the lines and areas to be printed. The plate is usually wiped with a ball of muslin or with the hand.

**Woodcut**
A method of relief printing where wood is the printing element. A wide variety of sharp cutting tools are usually used to form the design areas.

## Reproduction Credits

Lindsay Green, courtesy Tyler Graphics Ltd.: p. 2
Steven Sloman, courtesy Tyler Graphics Ltd.: pp. 11, 22, 26, 28, 29
Walker Art Center: pp. 4, 6, 9, 12, 14, 19, 23, 24, 25, 27

The exhibition *Prints from Tyler Graphics* has been generously supported by a grant from the National Endowment for the Arts. Additional support has come from The McKnight Foundation, the General Mills Foundation, The Bush Foundation, the Dayton Hudson Foundation for B. Dalton Bookseller, Dayton's and Target Stores, and the Minnesota State Arts Board.


Library of Congress Catalog Card Number: 84-51904
ISBN 0-935640-17-7

Dimensions in the captions are in inches; height precedes width.

## Staff for the Exhibition

**Director**
Martin Friedman

**Administration**
Donald C. Borrman

**Exhibition Curator**
Elizabeth Armstrong

**Curatorial Interns**
Fiona Irving
Nancy Roth

**Registration and Shipping**
Carolyn Clark DeCato
Jane Falk
Sharon Howell
Sheri Stearns

**Publication Design**
Donald Bergh
Robert Jensen

**Secretarial Assistance**
Laurie Skiba
Helen Slater

**Typesetting**
Julie Condecon

**Public Relations**
Mary Abbe Martin
Karen Statler

**Slide Tape Production**
Charles Helm
Elizabeth Josheff
Nancy Roth

**Photography**
Glenn Halvorson
Peter Latner

**Installation**
Hugh Jacobson
Mark Kramer
Mary Cutshall
David Dick
Steve Ecklund
Ron Elliott
Bradley Hudson
Joe Janson
Earl Kendall
David Lee
Dan Mackerman
Owen Osten
Josita Person
Tom Petraitas
Cody Riddle
John Snyder

## Board of Directors